CREATE OWN GROW

How to Create Enough For Your Life and Purpose

JOHN H. MORGAN

Publisher: People Prosper International
2650 FM 407 E Ste 145/150
Bartonville, Texas 76226
Phone: 505-634-9922

© Copyright 2021 John H. Morgan. All rights reserved.
Reproduction or translation of any part of this work without permission of the copyright owner is unlawful.
Requests for permission or further information should be addressed to: support@peopleprosper.org.

ISBN: 978-1-7378482-1-9

PEOPLEPROSPER.ORG

About the Author

Dr. John H. Morgan

John H. Morgan is an author, speaker, and the founder of People Prosper International. He is an executive coach through the John Morgan Company and a small business owner with MPI Property Investments. John has a Ph.D. in Organizational Leadership with an emphasis in Applied Economics from Regent University. He has a Master of Divinity from Denver Seminary, and he is an alumnus of Dallas Seminary. John pastored for 30 years, with 24 years as the Lead Pastor of Pinon Hills Community Church in Farmington, New Mexico. His hobbies are building projects, saltwater fishing, and cooking great food. He and Greg Lanee' Morgan have been married since 1984. They have five children and four grandchildren and live in the Dallas-Fort Worth area.

Acknowledgments

I would like to thank those who made this book possible:
- Kaley Morgan for graphic design.
- Carolina Florendo, Kristen Hallinan, Karissa Kellerstrass, Tim Hargrove, Jimmienell Morgan, and Steve Gamel for editing.
- Our PPI Program Partners around the world who connect us to countries, communities, and change-makers. Special thanks to Ronna Jordan, the Founder and Director of Houses with Hope, and to the Okello Family in Kenya; Shem Okello, The Honorable Member of Parliament, Jared Okello, Maddo Owino, and George Kienga. Thank you for your leadership in the Economic Empowerment Movement in Africa.
- Most of all, to God for his gifts and calling to empower the gifts and callings of others. *Pro Regno Suo* (For His Kingdom).

A Nonprofit Educational Organization Founded in 2016

SOLVING POVERTY THROUGH EMPOWERMENT

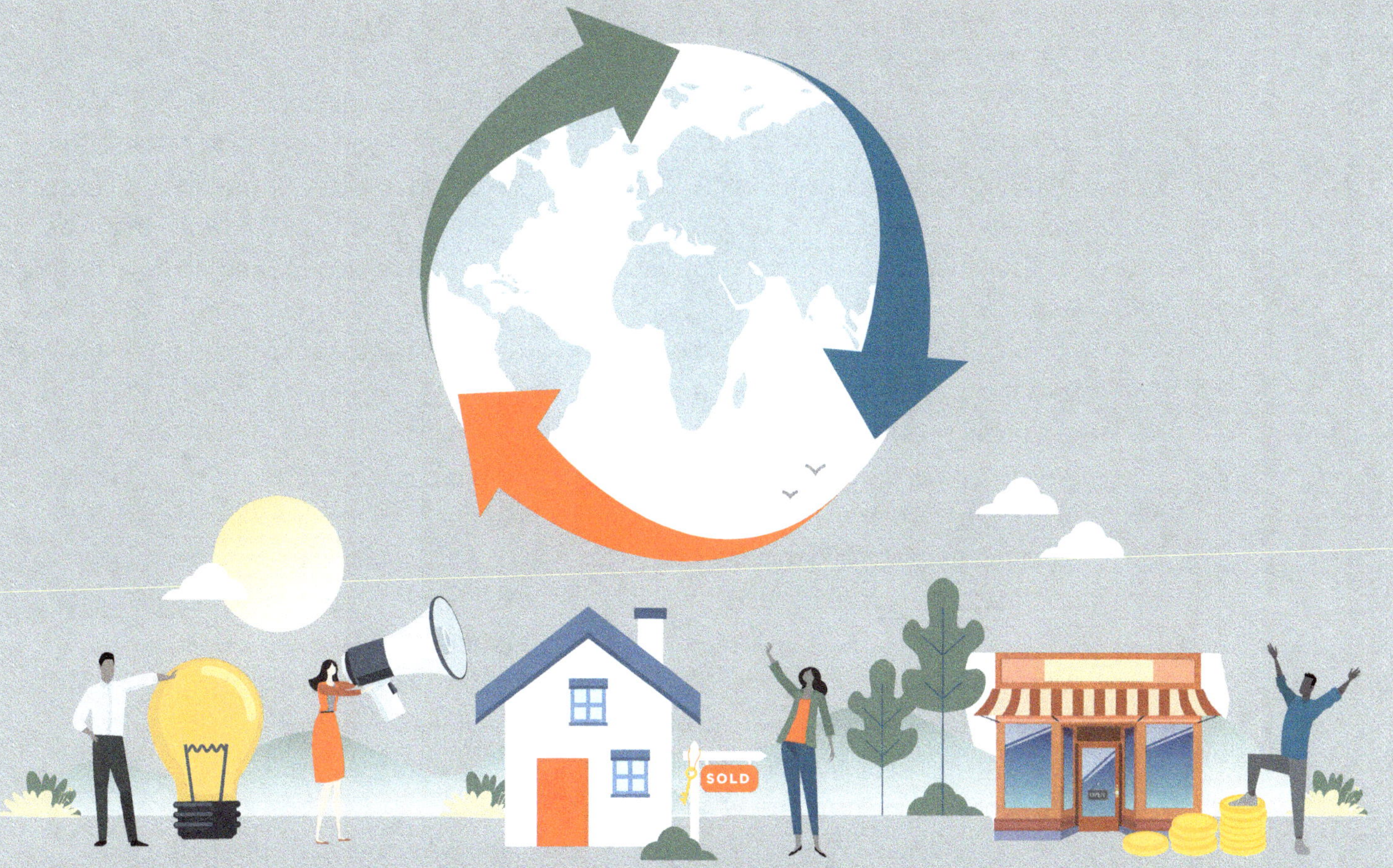

1 MILLION EMPOWERED BY 2030, 10 MILLION BY 2040, AND 100 MILLION BY 2050

peopleprosper.org

CREATE OWN GROW | ii

Introduction

At PPI, we call this book our PowerBook because it presents our most powerful ideas about Economic Empowerment and Economic Leadership in the most succinct and graphic way.

This book is our training manual that accompanies our Economic Empowerment and Economic Leadership Master Classes. The Master Classes are taught online on our website and they are taught live by our Certified PPI Trainers around the world.

We titled this book CREATE OWN GROW: *How to Create Enough for Your Life and Purpose* for two reasons. First, our African PPI partners began calling this course "CREATE OWN GROW," instead of Economic Empowerment and Economic Leadership, so we went with it. Second, the subtitle points out that this book and the courses are for anyone at any economic level seeking to have enough for their life and purpose. These principles and the practices work to solve poverty, create prosperity, and release people to live out their best purposes.

We present five foundational concepts on pages 1-6 to prepare your thinking for the teaching in this book. Like all foundations, the section is important for what follows.

The Economic Empowerment Master Class content makes up the majority of this book and is on pages 1-33. That section covers the principles, applications and practices of CREATE OWN GROW.

The Economic Leadership Master Class notes are on pages 34-36. This class teaches the Ten Conditions to Create a Culture of Prosperity. It is for those who want to be leaders who influence their communities and countries with growing prosperity.

There are testimonials of people whose lives have been changed by these Master Classes on pages 37-42.

Throughout the book, there are Q&A Notes that you can use to process the teaching. When you see a Pencil Icon you can go to the Q&A Notes in the back of the book on pages 43-48 to write your answers. You can use these Q&A Notes to learn the teaching content on your own, or, as we recommend, with a study group.

We are in the process of writing a full length book that teaches the content of our Economic Empowerment and Economic Leadership Master Classes. When it is available, we will post information about it under the Resources section of our website at peopleprosper.org.

You will understand this better after you have completed this book or the Master Classes, but for now, as you are proceeding through this material, we want to pronounce this blessing on you, "Go forth and conquer!"

People Prosper International's Model of Human Prosperity

CULTURAL EMPOWERMENT TRANSFORMATIONS

4 CULTURAL
THE TEN CONDITIONS THAT CREATE A CULTURE OF PROSPERITY

THE RESULTS OF PROSPERITY VS. POVERTY

3 BEHAVIORAL
RIGHT ACTIONS

2 MENTAL
TRUTH

1 SPIRITUAL
FAITH

PERSONAL EMPOWERMENT TRANSFORMATIONS

CREATE OWN GROW | iv

Glossary of Icons

 CREATE OWN GROW principles.

 CREATE the best value you can.

 OWN the best property you can.

 GROW the best business you can.

 Q&A Notes

 Economic Support

 Historic Support

 Biblical Support

 Testimonials

Table of Contents

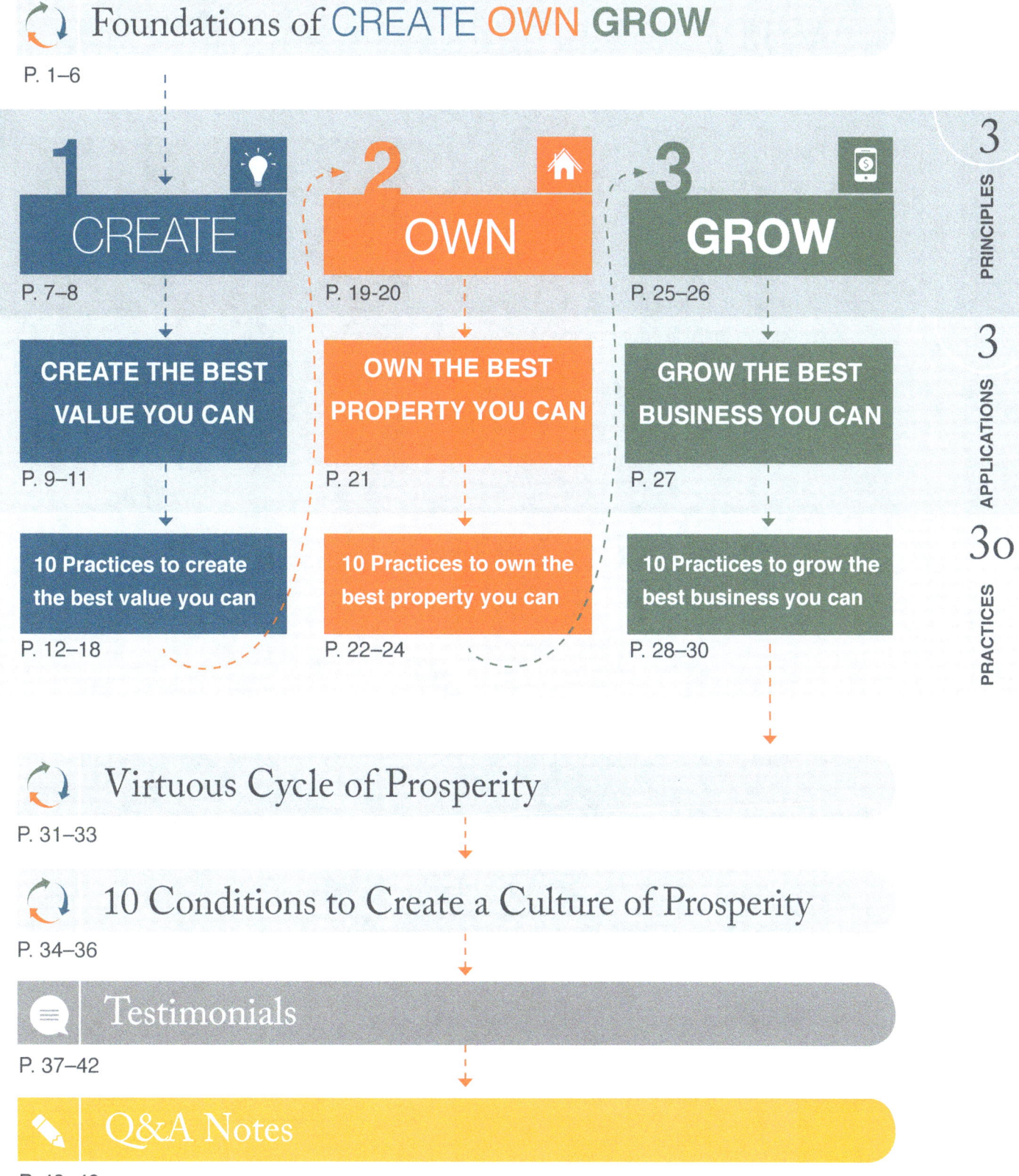

Foundations of
CREATE OWN GROW

1

WHY
THIS MATTERS

Poverty is a major problem that is destroying human health, security, peace, purpose, life, and dignity.

You were created for an important purpose, and you need to have enough resources to fulfill your purpose.

The world is changed when enough people fulfill their purpose to help others and make the world better.

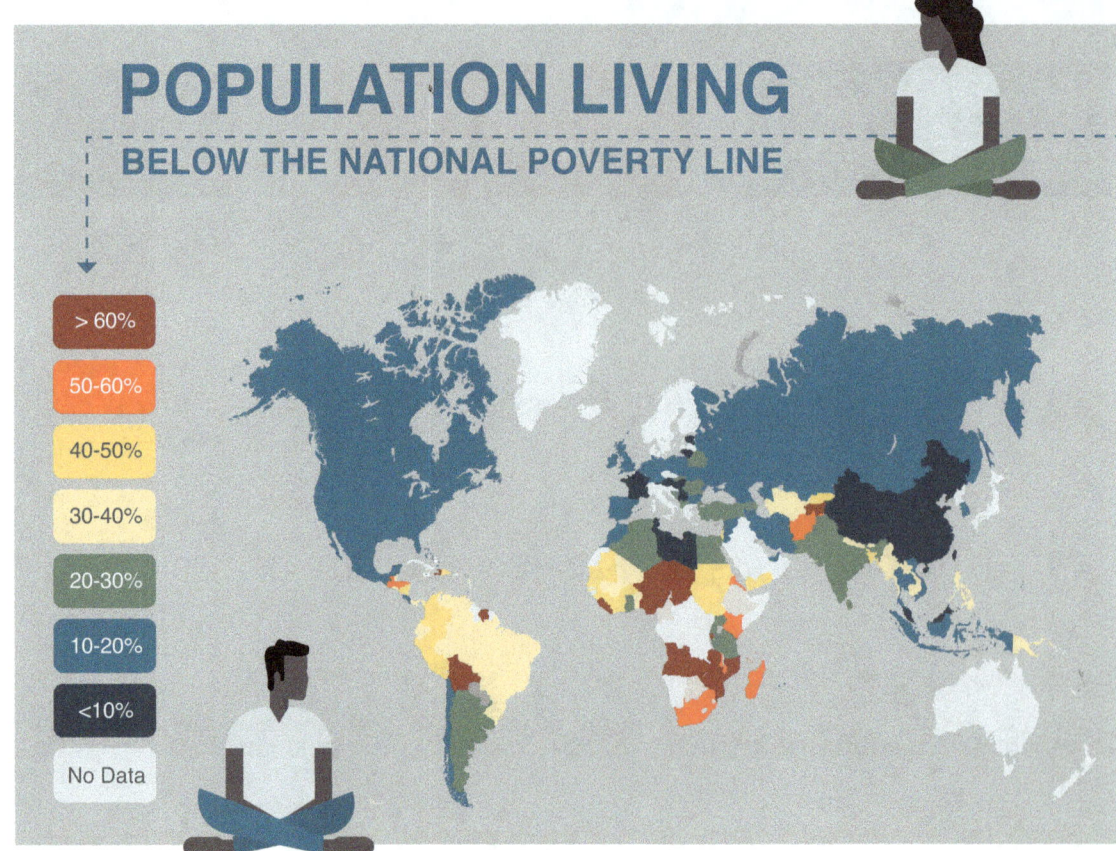

850 million people live in Extreme Poverty on less than $1.90 a day. Almost half of the world population lives in Regular Poverty, at risk of falling into Extreme Poverty. (https://www.worldbank.org/en/news/press-release/2020/10/07/covid-19-to-add-as-many-as-150-million-extreme-poor. Accessed 10.25.21)

Foundations

Are you willing to change your thinking?

- I am created to create value
- I am a future home owner
- I can run my own business
- I can create my own wealth
- I believe in myself
- I can be successful

THE QUESTION IS, "ARE YOU READY TO CHANGE YOUR THINKING TO ACHIEVE BETTER RESULTS?"

HOW
TO CHANGE THE RESULTS

To change the results you are getting, you must change your actions. To change your actions, you must change your thinking.

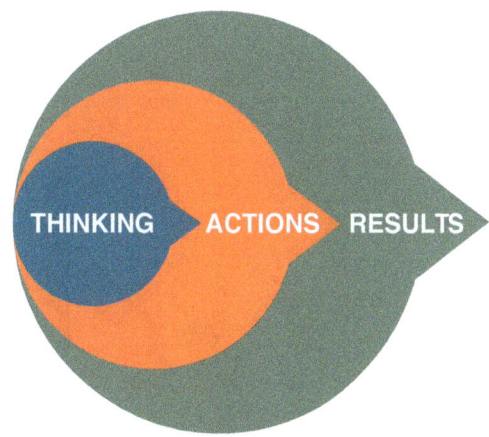

The Cognitive Model

The bottom line is this: To solve your poverty or to grow your prosperity, you will have to change how and what you think about some things. Many of the results you have been getting have been caused by your actions or inactions. Many of the actions or inactions that you have been doing are the results of the ways you have been thinking.

CREATE OWN GROW will challenge you to learn some new things, believe some new things, and do new things that are different from what you and the people with whom you associate have believed and done in the past. And you are going to get new and better results.

Foundations

3

THE SOURCES
OF THE CREATE OWN GROW **PRINCIPLES ARE ECONOMICS, HISTORY, AND THE BIBLICAL WORLDVIEW**

 **IMPORTANT ECONOMIC WORKS SUPPORT THE PRINCIPLES OF** CREATE OWN GROW

TOP FOUR RECOMMENDATIONS

 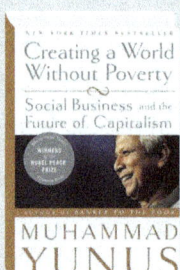 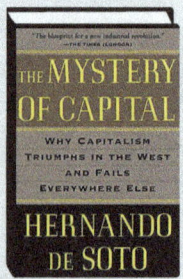 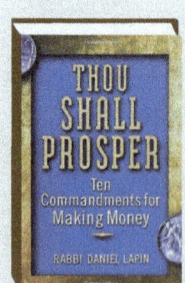

Michael Novak, ***The Spirit of Democratic Capitalism***, 1982

Muhammad Yunnis, ***Creating a World Without Poverty***, 1998

Hernando DeSoto, ***The Mystery of Capital***, 2000

Rabbi Daniel Lapin, ***Thou Shall Prosper***, 2002

Foundations

- John Locke, **Two Treatises on Government**, 1689. (The most important political/economic philosophical & theological thought leadership behind the U.S. Declaration of Independence & Constitution).
- Adam Smith, **The Wealth of Nations**, 1776.
- Max Weber, **The Protestant Ethic and the Spirit of Capitalism**, 1905 German/1930 English.
- F.A. Hayek, **The Road to Serfdom**, 1944.
- Milton Friedman, **Free to Choose**, 1980.
- Thomas Sowell, **Basic Economics**, 2000.
- Rodney Stark, **The Victory of Reason**, 2005.
- Robert Sirico, **Defending the Free Market**, 2010.
- Acton Institute's video documentary, **Poverty Cure**, 2012.
- John Morgan, **The Spirit of Human Prosperity**, 2020.

More Good Resources

 **HISTORY** ILLUSTRATES THAT THE PRINCIPLES OF CREATE OWN GROW ARE THE PATH TO PROSPERITY

- The Free World v. Socialist Dictatorships.
- Singapore v. Cuba since 1959.
- Israel v. Surrounding Countries.
- The Heritage Foundation's Index of Economic Freedom demonstrates how the freedom to CREATE OWN GROW is the path to national and individual prosperity.

 THE **BIBLICAL WORLDVIEW** TEACHES IT

- God is The Creator of all things: both the material and spiritual worlds. He has established the principles of how both work. (Colossians 1:16)
- God, The Creator, created us in His image to create new value on earth to earn our livings, to benefit others, to make the world a better place, and to honor Him. (Genesis 1:27-28)
- God gave His people property rights for their security and prosperity in this material world.
(Genesis 12:7 & 20:15)

- Business done properly is a righteous activity because it is the creation of new value through products, services, and solutions. (Matthew 15:14-30)

CREATE OWN GROW | 4

Foundations

4

OUR DEFINITIONS
OF POVERTY AND PROSPERITY ARE ESSENTIAL TO UNDERSTANDING THE PRINCIPLES OF CREATE OWN GROW

pov·er·ty /pävərdē/
(noun) lacking the ability to create enough for your life and purpose.

pros·per·i·ty /präˈsperədē/
(noun) having the ability to create enough for your life and purpose.

CREATE OWN GROW is not teaching materialism. We do not believe the purpose of life is to make money and acquire things. We believe the purpose of life is to serve God and to serve people according to His purpose for our lives.

We only need enough for our lives and purposes. Your good purposes determine the amounts you need.

People who do not create their own resources for their lives are essentially poor and unempowered. They must rely on the value created by others.

5 | PEOPLEPROSPER.ORG

Foundations

GATHER

AN EMPOWERMENT GROUP TO STUDY THE CREATE OWN GROW PRINCIPLES.

The best way to learn the CREATE OWN GROW principles is to gather an empowerment group and study the Master Classes together. Meet at a regular time and place to watch and discuss one lesson at a time.

WWW.PEOPLEPROSPER.ORG to attend the Master Classes and download the class notes.

GET A FLASH DRIVE with Master Classes and Materials from a PPI Trainer.

prin·ci·ple /ˈprinsəpəl/
(noun) a universal law of cause and effect.

prac·tice /ˈprak-təs/
(verb) an action to apply a principle.

- Principles reveal what causes what, such as what causes poverty and what causes prosperity.
- Principles apply to everyone, everywhere, and across history.
- Practices may change, but principles never do.

The Foundations of CREATE OWN GROW

1 Poverty is a major problem, and you were created for a purpose.

2 You must change your thinking to change your results.

3 The principles are based on economics, history, and biblical worldview.

4 Poverty is lacking the ability to create. Prosperity is having the ability to create.

5 Learn CREATE OWN GROW with an empowerment group.

CREATE OWN GROW | 6

Principle #1: Create
Value is Created

ECONOMIC SUPPORT

Value, money, resources, wealth, and prosperity are created when people do work that creates products, services, and solutions that people need and want. **This is where wealth is born.**

HISTORIC SUPPORT

The wealth of nations is generated by the value created by their people in products, services, and solutions. The currencies of nations are strong or weak based on the value created by their people.

See the Index of Economic Freedom from The Heritage Foundation.

Let's Get Practical!

When we create a new valued product, service, or solution, we create value that did not exist before.

- The iron worker creates an iron product or structure that did not exist.
- The livestock shepherd or herder creates more and better livestock.
- The farmer creates more and better produce than what would have existed.
- The engineer creates a bridge, airplane, or computer that did not exist before.
- The teacher creates an educated student who was not educated before.

Principle: Create

 BIBLICAL SUPPORT

God the Creator created us in His image and placed us on this earth to continue the work of creating a world where we can make our livings, bless our fellow man, make the world a better place, and honor Him.

- *So God created man in His own image, in the image and likeness of God He created him; male and female He created them. And God blessed them and said to them, "Be fruitful, multiply, and fill the earth, and subdue it [using all its vast resources in the service of God and man]; and have dominion over the fish of the sea, the birds of the air, and over every living creature that moves upon the earth."* (Genesis 1:27-28 The Amplified Bible)
- Part of the image and likeness of God in man is the ability to create new things on earth that have new value.
- The first humans were given the job of making the Garden of Eden better. (Genesis 2:15)
- Their children created new value in agriculture and livestock. (Genesis 4:2)
- The next generations worked in agriculture, manufacturing, and the arts. (Genesis 4:20-22)
- Abraham, the father of the Jews, Christians, and Muslims, by faith, created value in a very large livestock business. He became very wealthy by creating it through sheep, goats, oxen, camels, and donkeys. (Genesis 13:2)
- The Law of Moses was the original Constitution for the nation of Israel in ancient times. It contained principles and practices of CREATE OWN GROW.
- The historic legacy of Judaism and Christianity has been to create prosperity through a worldview of CREATE OWN GROW wherever it has had a critical mass of influence.

Application of Create
Create the Best Value You Can

You are the best source of your own prosperity. You can use your talents, abilities, and interests to create products, services, and solutions to meet your own needs and the needs of others.

If you don't create your own prosperity, then you are dependent upon others to do so. There is satisfaction and fulfillment in creating the value that makes our livings because it is part of the purpose for which God created us.

The poor are not the problem. They are the solution. They have the talents that can be put to work to create the value to create the income they need. What they need is empowerment. They need the knowledge and skills to create the resources they need. (Poverty Cure, Documentary Videos by the Acton Institute)

> THERE IS MORE POTENTIAL WEALTH IN THE TALENTS OF THE PEOPLE OF A NATION THAN IN ALL THE NATURAL RESOURCES IN THEIR LAND.
>
> —POVERTY CURE,
>   Documentary Video Series by the Acton Institute, 2012.

The income you make is determined by the value you create.

The issue is not just how **hard** we work, it is also how **high** we work. We have to create a high enough value to receive a high enough income for our lives and purposes.

Ask Yourself...

- What are my strengths and abilities?
- Which can help me create the most value?

Application: Create

Use Your Best Abilities, Talents, and Skills →  to → **Meet People's Greatest Needs**

 Teach

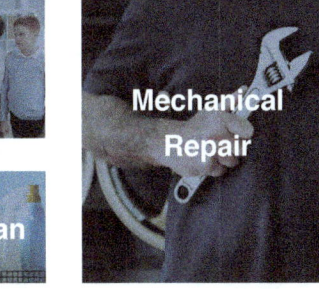 Mechanical Repair

 Transportation

 Education

 Cook | Clean

 Clothes | Shoes

 Manage & Supervise

 Artistic Expression

 Religion

 Sports

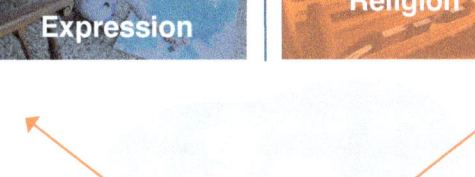

 Music  Writing

 Grow 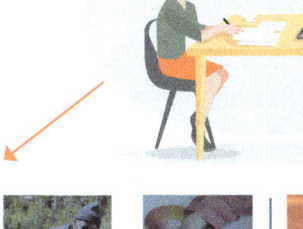 Design

 Fitness  Water

 Food  Shelter

Other Abilities, Talents, and Skills: Make, Sell, Transport, Analysis, Research, Data Management, Negotiating, Coaching, Financial Management, Innovation, Audio/Video Production, Computer Skills, Strategic Planning, Leadership, Counseling, Empathy, Translating, Cross-cultural Relationships, Organize, Communications, Decorate.

Other Needs: Entertainment, Health, Art, Leisure, Fun, Medical Care, Health Products, News, Economic Empowerment, Financial Knowledge, Financial Services, Rest and Recreation, Music, Purpose, Safety, Literacy, Work Skills, Household Goods.

Ask Yourself...

I will use ___(Which ability, talent, and skill?)___ in order to ___(Which need do I want to meet?)___.

CREATE OWN GROW | 10

10 Practices of Create
How to Create the Best Value You Can

1

RAISE

YOUR IMAGE OF YOURSELF:
THINK OF YOURSELF AS A VALUE CREATOR

If you have a job, go to work focused on the value you will create for your boss, the organization that you work for, and your customers.

If you are self-employed, keep thinking of better ways to create value for your customers.

If you are looking for a job, on your resume and in the interview explain what kind of value you will be creating for your boss, your company, and your customers.

Look for problems and solve them because all work is problem solving.

Do not...	Do...
... think of yourself as a time-spender. No one cares about your time, except you. The value you bring to your job is the value you create.	... maximize your time by creating the best value you can.
... think of yourself as a position-filler. Your job title is not your value.	... use the position you have to look for the best problems you can solve.
... think of yourself as a space-taker. Sitting at a desk, in a vehicle, or standing at a counter or a job site has no value in itself.	... go into every space you occupy and look for problems to solve and value to create.
...think of yourself as entitled to take, bribe, or steal whatever you can for yourself, your family, and your friends.	... think of yourself as entrusted to protect the property of your workplace.
... think of yourself as a consumer. Your greatest activity in the economy is not consumption; it is creation. People can create far more than they consume, otherwise we would have depleted the earth a long time ago. Cancer is a consumer. Rats are consumers. Cockroaches are consumers.	... think of yourself as a value creator.

The Poor Sell Time. The Wealthy Sell Value.

When you do more that you're paid to do, eventually you will be paid more for what you do.
—Zig Ziglar

Practices: Create

REPLACE
THE ZERO SUM FALLACY IN YOUR MIND WITH THE GROWING VALUE TRUTH

Zero Sum Fallacy:
The false idea that the money, value, wealth, and prosperity in the world is a static non-growing amount, which means the only way you can get what you need is to take it from other people who have it. The Zero Sum Fallacy produces **envy**.

Growing Value Truth:
The truth that new money, value, wealth, and prosperity in the world is constantly being created by those who create new products, services, and solutions, which means the best way to get what you need is to create it. The Growing Value Truth produces **ambition**.

en·vy /ˈenvē/
(noun) a sinful desire for what others have.

am·bi·tion /amˈbiSH(ə)n/
(noun) a righteous desire to create value.

Action:
Choose daily to mentally place yourself in the outer dynamic ring of the economy where you are creating new value, instead of inside the old static circle of the economy where you focus on the possessions of others.

Ask Yourself...
- What possession of others have I been envying?
- What value would I love to create?

Practices: Create

3 RAISE
YOUR EFFORT

Work Harder. If you are not bringing your full energies and efforts to your work, then start working harder. Look harder for the problems you can solve. Then work harder to solve them. You deserve the rewards of your full engagement to create value.

Work Smarter. Don't just work harder at low-level work that cannot pay enough for what you need. Work smarter by choosing work that uses the best abilities you have to meet the greatest needs that people have. If you need to raise your skills, get some training or coaching on how to do higher work.

Work Six. Work a maximum of six days in a row, then take a day off for rest. God designed our spirits, our minds, our bodies, and the world for a cycle of work and rest to be able to do our best work and to live our best lives.

> SIX DAYS YOU SHALL LABOR AND DO ALL YOUR WORK, BUT THE SEVENTH DAY IS A SABBATH TO THE LORD YOUR GOD. ON IT, YOU SHALL NOT DO ANY WORK...
>
> —EXODUS 20:9

4 RAISE
YOUR PEOPLE SKILLS

The reason people often fail in jobs is not because they lack the technical knowledge and skills of the work. It is **because they do not have good people skills**. Those who have good people skills, and technical knowledge and skills, are the ones who succeed.

> AND LOOK OUT FOR ONE ANOTHER'S INTERESTS, NOT JUST FOR YOUR OWN.
>
> —PHILIPPIANS 2:4

People Skills You Must Master

- Confidence vs. insecurity
- Cause no harm
- Recognize others
- Ask people about themselves
- Introduce yourself
- Remember/Use people's names
- Affirm others
- Help others succeed

You can get what you want in life if you help others get what they want.

—Zig Ziglar

Practices: Create

5

RAISE
YOUR VISION, AMBITION, AND ACTION PLAN

There are several questions to ask yourself and to answer in writing to raise your vision, ambition, and to create your action plan.

Dream big, but... never hope for anything more than you work for.

Ask Yourself...

- What are the best talents and abilities that I have?
- What is the biggest need that people have that I would most like to meet?
- What knowledge and skills would I be willing to learn to be able to do this?
- **VISION:** Describe what my life could look like one year or more in the future if I pursued these things.
- **AMBITION:** Describe the value I would like to create for others and that I would be creating for myself and my family with better income.
- **MY ACTION PLAN:** What are the three main action steps I will take in the next few years to make my vision and ambition happen?
  - Step 1:
  - Step 2:
  - Step 3:

vi·sion /ˈviZHən/
(noun) the picture inside your head of what your life situation could be in the future.

am·bi·tion /amˈbiSH(ə)n/
(noun) a righteous desire to create value.

ac·tion plan
/ˈakSH(ə)n plan/ (noun) the three main action steps you can take to pursue your vision and ambition.

This is Your Action Plan: EVERY DAY, do some ACTION to make progress on your plan!

CREATE OWN GROW | 14

Practices: Create

6 RAISE
YOUR INTEGRITY

Most employers cannot find employees whom they can trust with managing:
- Their time to stay productive.
- Other people properly.
- The property and equipment of the business.
- The supplies of the business.
- The confidential information of the business.
- The money of the business.

Someday, you may own a business where you need people with integrity whom you can trust. Having integrity now makes you promotable, and it will prepare you to run your own business. **Integrity is one of the greatest values you can create.**

in·teg·ri·ty /inˈtegrədē/
(noun) doing what you agree to do.

a·gree·ment /əˈgrēmənt/ (noun) a mutual decision, position or arrangement.

trust /trəst/
(noun) belief in the integrity of another.

> Trust in the integrity of those who make agreements is the basis of good relationships and a good society.

7 RAISE
YOUR RESPONSIBILITY

7 General Levels of Responsbility in Organizations

- Be the Top Leader of several organizations.
- Be the Top Leader of an organization.
- Be a General Manager of several managers.
- Manage a location or a department in an organization.
- Supervise a crew or a shift of people effectively.
- Create the outcomes your boss needs without being told how.
- Do the tasks well that your boss assigns you to do.

Higher levels of effective responsibility usually result in higher levels of pay. Seek the highest level you can do well without feeling overwhelmed.

Practices: Create

RAISE
YOUR KNOWLEDGE AND SKILLS

Every kind of work has its specialized body of knowledge and skills that can be learned through formal education, self-learning, and experience. The more knowledge and skills you have for that work, the more value you can create and the more money you can make.

know·ledge /ˈnäləj/
(noun) what is true about a particular kind of work.

skill /skil/
(noun) the actions you can do that create value in a kind of work that makes money.

The people who create the highest value and make the most money are life-long learners who constantly ask, "What knowledge and skills do I need to learn next?"

Ask Yourself...

- What knowledge and skills do I need to learn next?

3 Types of Knowledge and Skills to Learn:

1. Technical knowledge and skills of a certain industry or work sector.

2. People skills to work well with others.

3. Leadership knowledge and skills to lead yourself and others well.

CREATE OWN GROW | 16

Practices: Create

9 RAISE
YOUR HEART AND YOUR FINANCIAL HEALTH: TITHE AND SAVE

 GIVE

Give some of your income to:
- Your Church
- A Nonprofit Organization that does good work
- People who are in need

 SAVE

Save some of your income:
- Do not spend more than you have or more than you make
- Avoid debt and payoff your debts
- Create a spending plan to control where your money goes

 GROW YOUR WEALTH

Grow Your Giving and your Savings to 10% each of Your Income. The 10-10-80 Plan.

10-10-80
GIVING SAVING LIVING

> Go be the ant, o sluggard, observe her ways and be wise, which, having no chief, officer, or ruler, prepares her food in the summer and gathers her provision in the harvest. —Proverbs 6:6–8

> Honor the LORD with your wealth, with the firstfruits of all your crops; then your barns will be filled to overflowing, and your vats will brim over with new wine.
> —Proverbs 3:9–10

Giving does 3 things

1. It makes you a bigger and better person on the inside because it puts money in its place in your life, it affirms that everything is God's and comes from God, and it affirms that God will bless you to create more.
2. It moves God to bless your work and your finances.
3. It joins God's work to fund the Church, ministries, and works that support you spiritually and that bless others.

Saving does 3 things

1. It teaches you to control your money instead of your money controlling you.
2. It protects you when you have financial emergencies.
3. It provides for you with future opportunities to buy better things and to put money to work as capital.

Practices: Create

START
A SIDE HUSTLE OR A BUSINESS

10

Ask Yourself...

Do I have a job? yes → Do I make enough money? yes →
no ↓   no ↓

no ↓ Start a Business or Side Hustle. Do I know how? yes →

1. Identify my strengths and talents: **What can I do well?**
2. Identify what I want to do: **What kind of work do I want to do?**
3. Identify a need that people have: **What will people pay for?**
4. **Pick a business** that fits my talents and desires and a need people have.
5. **Start where I am and with what I have.** Don't assume you need to spend a lot of money or get a loan for expensive things to start. **Bootstrap it.** That means make the most of the resources you have now to create some new value.

↓

Do you need ideas? no →

yes ↓

Side hustles & small businesses that have been bootstrapped to make new money:

Manufacturing	Farm & Food	Selling Products	Selling Services	Education & Care
gates, doors, furniture, clothes, shelves, kayaks, etc.	chicken and goat raising, fish farming, cafe, vegetable gardens, cooking and selling food, catering, grocery store, making cookies, sauces, spices, etc.	selling scarves, accessories, filtered water, arts, crafts, buying and selling good used clothes, leather goods, furniture, etc.	cleaning, handyman, painting, home construction, delivery, yard work, mechanic work, welding, computer or assistant services	daycare, elderly care, starting a school in a home, teaching art, starting a fitness business outdoors, dog sitting, dog walking, home rentals

CREATE OWN GROW | 18

Principle #2: Own
Property Preserves Prosperity

 ECONOMIC SUPPORT

Property transforms money into capital. Two almost magical things happen when we do two things:

First, when we create a useful product, service, or solution, we create new value that did not exist before – we create new mone, value, and prosperity.

Second, when we take some of the money we create and use it to buy property, we create a kind of capital that did not exist before.

cap·i·tal /kapədl/
(noun) a resource you can put to work to make money.

Let's Get Practical!

Property is a unique and powerful kind of capital because of its power to help us create **multiple values** at the **same time**.

- It can be a place for us to live.
- It has value that will probably grow over time.
- It is a place where we can create products, services, and solutions.
- It is a place where we may be able to conduct a business.
- It may be a place where we can grow a garden, farm crops, or raise livestock.
- It may be a place where we can gather resources: water, wood, minerals.
- It may be a place where we can gain rents.
- It is a place where you can store goods: vehicles, equipment, tools, products, supplies, valuables, etc.
- We may get a loan against it to start a business or to buy another property.

19 | PEOPLEPROSPER.ORG

Principle: Own

HISTORIC SUPPORT

The difference between the prosperous of the world and the poor is that the prosperous have fairly straight forward ways to legally own property, which gives them the power to create wealth, while and the poor do not.
(Hernando DeSoto, *The Mystery of Capital*.)

Hernando De Soto, Peruvian Economist & Global Expert on Solving Poverty

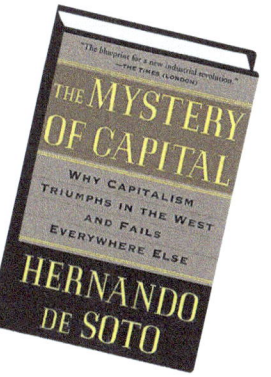

BIBLICAL SUPPORT

Property rights were codified in the Old Testament of the Bible and Christian thought. Both of these promoted property rights as sacred. (John Locke, *Two Treatises*.)

- God insisted that Israel be a landed people for their security and prosperity. (Genesis 12:7)
- The Old Testament Law codified property rights. (Exodus 20:15)
- Christian economic influence promoted property rights. (Rodney Stark, *The Victory of Reason*.)

The Problem

CASH HAS WINGS.

Nothing disappears faster than cash because we and our families have constant needs and desires. To preserve wealth, we need to own something that has lasting value, that can be used to create new value, and that is not easily spent on our immediate needs. Owning property can accomplish these things.

Legal Ownership of Property is Required to Preserve Prosperity

- It has to be owned with a legal **deed**.
- The **courts** must enforce your property rights.
- This protects the owner, and it turns the owner's money into **capital**.

CREATE OWN GROW | 20

Application of Own
Own the Best Property You Can

HOMES   **RENTAL PROPERTIES**

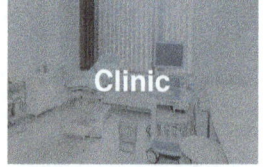

BUSINESSES   **FARMS/AGRICULTURE**   **ORGANIZATIONS**

Ask Yourself

- What kind of property do I want to own?

10 Practices of Own
How to Own the Best Property You Can

1

THINK

OF YOURSELF AS A FUTURE PROPERTY OWNER

- Know you are worthy of ownership.
- Decide you will not rent forever.
- Make ownership a life goal.
- Make ownership a generational goal for your family.

2

THINK

OF PROPERTY OWNERSHIP AS A WAY TO GROW PROSPERITY

- Know that good property ownership at the right time builds prosperity.
- Property is a unique kind of capital that creates multiple kinds of value at the same time.
- Good property generally grows in value over time.
- Good property ownership is a key difference between the poor and the prosperous.

3

SET

YOUR GOALS AND PLANS TO OWN PROPERTY

- Write a goal for when you want to own property.
- Create the best value you can to create the best income you can.
- Budget your spending to save money to buy a property.

Ask Yourself

- When will I own property?
- Am I creating the best value I can to create the best income I can?
- Am I budgeting? If not, I will create a budget and use it.

CREATE OWN GROW | 22

Practices: Own

4 **ELIMINATE**
YOUR DEBT BY PAYING IT OFF

5 **SAVE**
MONEY TO BUY PROPERTY

6 **LOOK**
FOR A GOOD PROPERTY TO BUY

Ask Yourself

- How can I create value from my home?
    - Growing a garden
    - Raising livestock
    - Conducting business
    - Renting a portion of it to tenants
    - Home improvements
    - Home expansions

- It is worth the price & you can afford it.
- It can be a home for you.
- It should grow in value over time.
- You can improve it.
- **There are multiple ways you can create value from your home.**

7 **BUY**
YOUR FIRST PROPERTY
- With cash, or
- With a down payment and a loan from a loan company (Bank, Mortgage Co., Credit Union, Sacco, etc..), or
- With a down payment and a loan from the property seller.

Practices: Own

MAINTAIN
AND IMPROVE YOUR PROPERTY

- Keep your property in good repair.
- Make improvements: new interior features, new furnishings, remodel.
- Build new space onto an existing building.
- Build more buildings on the property.
- Add property features: landscaping, drives, storage buildings, workshops, rental space.

Ask Yourself

- What property maintenance and improvements do I need to do?

8

CONSIDER
SELLING YOUR PROPERTY TO BUY A BETTER ONE

9

INVEST
YOUR EQUITY

- To start or grow a business.
- To buy an investment property that you can sell for a higher price with some time or some improvements.
- To buy a house, business, or farm property to rent out to tenants.
- To buy a property for your business.

10

eq·ui·ty /ˈekwədē/
(noun) The value of your property minus the debt you owe on it.

TOTAL VALUE OF HOME — $100,000
EQUITY — $60,000
MORTGAGE — $40,000

CREATE OWN GROW | 24

Principle #3: Grow
Business Multiplies Prosperity

 ECONOMIC SUPPORT

Business multiplies prosperity because it puts multiple kinds of capital to work together to create value versus just the labor of one person.

1. People
2. Specialized Knowledge
3. Supplies
4. Tools and Equipment
5. Property
6. Money

Your Personal Labor is Economic Addition

You are adding new value through the products, services, and solutions you are creating. When you work for an employer, you are adding value to your life with your income.

Business is Economic Multiplication

It puts multiple kinds of capital to work to create multiplied value.

Principle: Grow

HISTORIC SUPPORT

The pro-business nations have been the most prosperous because they encourage the engine of prosperity.

Business is the economic engine that funds the institutions of human prosperity.

Since 1959...
Singapore pursued pro-business policies. Now singapore is #1 in per capita wealth.

Since 1959...
Cuba pursued anti-business socialist/ communist policies. Cuba is one of the poorest nations in the Western hemisphere.

Singapore

Cuba

BIBLICAL SUPPORT

Business done properly is one of the most righteous things one can do. It creates human prosperity.

- Abraham, the Spiritual Patriarch of Judaism, Islam, and Christianity, was a very wealthy and successful businessman. (Genesis 12:16, 13:3, & 14:14)
- Jesus affirmed the righteous essence of business in the Parable of the Talents in Matthew 25:14-30.
- St. Paul practiced a trade business and commanded Christians to work to earn their livings instead of scheming to get other people's money. (II Thessalonians 3:6-18)

Application of Grow
Grow the Best Business You Can

If you work for a government agency or a nonprofit organization, support pro-business policies to keep the economic engine growing.

Start a side hustle.

Grow your own business.

Work for a business and help it succeed.

Expand your business with more locations.

Ask Yourself

- Which of these business options fit my skillset and passions the best?

Invest money in businesses.

Own and grow several businesses.

27 | PEOPLEPROSPER.ORG

10 Practices of Grow
How to Grow the Best Business You Can

THINK — 1

OF YOURSELF AS A BUSINESS OWNER

- First, realize that you are in business even if your business is to sell your time and talents to an employer. Understand you are working for Your Business. Your business will grow as you intentionally grow the value it and you create.
- Second, know that business done properly is one of the most righteous things you can do.
- Third, know you are worthy of owning a business. God has created you in his image with gifts and talents to create value and to put the resources of His world to work to create value. (Genesis 1:28)

MAKE — 2

A PLAN TO OWN AND GROW A BUSINESS

- Decide what your product, service, or solution will be.
- Will you improve on another business model or create an original model?
- Decide what unique value your business will provide that will make your business successful.
- Decide if this will be a side hustle or a full-time business.
- Try to bootstrap it first (see pg 18). Do not get a loan for an unproven business.
- Write a plan of how you will do this business.

The way to get started is to quit talking and begin doing — Walt Disney

Ask Yourself

- What is my Unique Value Proposition (UVP)?
- Where and when will I do this business?
- How will I get the supplies and resources I need?
- How will I get people to help?
- How will I let customers know about my business?

Test, learn, and adjust your business plans as you go.

UVP: What you do better than anyone else.

CREATE   OWN   GROW | 28

Practices: Grow

3 <mark>START</mark>
YOUR BUSINESS

4 <mark>IMPROVE</mark>
YOUR PEOPLE, PRODUCTS, SERVICES AND SOLUTIONS

5 <mark>IMITATE</mark>
WHAT IS WORKING ELSEWHERE AND DO IT BETTER

6 <mark>INVENT</mark>
NEW PRODUCTS, SERVICES, AND SOLUTIONS

7 <mark>EXPAND</mark>
YOUR BUSINESS CAPACITY

Ask Yourself

- How can I improve my people, products, services, and solutions?
- What is working elsewhere and how can I do it better?
- What new products, services, and solutions can I create?
- How can I expand my business capacity? Add key people? Add equipment? Add more space? Add a new location in a new market?

If you have enough demand that you could sell more with greater capacity, then invest in growing your capacity. **This is the time when getting a business loan makes the most sense, when you are expanding a proven business.**

- Structure your business properly to put capable people at the right levels of responsibility.
- Add key people you need to create more.
- Add equipment you need to create more.
- Add space you need to create more.
- Add a new location in a new market.

Practices: Grow

EXPAND
YOUR BUSINESS DEMAND

8

If you could produce more if you had greater demand, then invest in growing your demand:
- Do a better job of defining, delivering, and selling your Unique Value Proposition. (UVP: What you do better than anyone else).
- Do a better job of marketing – letting people know about your business and your UVP.
- Sell, sell, sell. Nothing sells itself. The greatest ideas in the world and the greatest businesses in the world are driven by selling.

CREATE
A NEW BUSINESS

9

If you have a strong idea and desire to start another business, then do it:
- Know your role will change to directional leadership over multiple businesses.
- Know that the success of multiple business lies in your ability to get managers of each business who manage them well.

INVEST
IN BUSINESS

10

- Invest in businesses by loaning money to people and businesses you believe in.
- Invest in business stock funds via an investment brokerage or financial institution.

Virtuous Cycle of Prosperity

First Cycle

11. Start with what you have in knowledge, skills, opportunities, and resources and start the best business you can.
12. Keep learning and changing as needed to grow the best business that you want.
13. If it is worth it, get a loan based on the value of your first property to grow your business:
    - Add employees
    - Add equipment
    - Expand your land or building space
    - Add locations
    - Increase sales

START HERE

1. Learn the principles of CREATE OWN GROW.
2. Look for ways to create more value.
3. Raise your effort.
4. Raise your knowledge and skill in a kind of work where you can create more value.
5. Make more money by creating more value.
6. Save money to buy your first property.

7. Look for a good property to buy:
   - You can live there
   - You can improve it
   - It will grow in value
   - You can create other values there
   - You can afford it
8. Buy your first property with cash or with a down payment and payments you can afford.
9. Improve your property and create value there:
   - Grow vegetables
   - Grow livestock
   - Rent part of it out
   - Do business there
10. Save money to start a business.

A **Vicious** Cycle is a circle of activities that keep making your situation worse. An example is depression leading to alcoholism leading to losing employment. It is a downward spiral.

A **Virtuous** Cycle is a circle of activities that keep making your situation better. An example is gaining new skills, which leads to better employment, which leads to owning property.

Virtuous Cycle of Prosperity

Next Cycles

3. With your added income and wealth, you can now expand your business, start new businesses, buy businesses, or invest in businesses.

1. Your previous cycle of CREATE OWN GROW is causing you to create the best value you can and to make the most money that you can.

2. With your added prosperity, you can now buy more properties for your business, income, and investments.

CONTINUE REPEATING THE CYCLE, AND EACH TIME DO IT BETTER AND BIGGER THAN BEFORE.

CREATE   OWN   GROW | 32

Virtuous Cycle of Prosperity

Cycle of Generational Prosperity

3. Teach and show your children how to grow the best business they can.

1. Teach and show your children how to create the best value they can.

2. Teach and show your children how to own the best property they can.

CREATE A FAMILY CULTURE OF PROSPERITY AND HAND DOWN GENERATIONAL WEALTH.

Economic Leadership
10 Conditions to Create a Culture of Prosperity

1. A CRITICAL MASS

OF PEOPLE IN THE COMMUNITY KNOW AND PRACTICE THE PRINCIPLES OF CREATE OWN GROW

- There is a strong and influential group of people who keep the movement of CREATE OWN GROW alive and growing in the community.

2. THE THREE PILLAR FREEDOMS

OF A FREE AND JUST SOCIETY ARE IN PLACE: RELIGIOUS FREEDOM, POLITICAL FREEDOM, AND ECONOMIC FREEDOM

- Religious Freedom is the right and freedom to practice any religion or non-religion whose practice does not violate good laws that protect others from harm.
- Political Freedom is the classic freedoms of democratic self-governance.
- Economic Freedom is the freedom to practice the Principles of CREATE OWN GROW without government or other interference.

3. MARRIAGE & CHILD RAISING

IN FAMILIES IS A CULTURAL VALUE

- The marriage dividend is the economic benefit of married couples cooperating for an economically stronger household that practices CREATE OWN GROW.
- Children raised in a loving and supportive home and who are taught to practice the Principles of CREATE OWN GROW will be productive and prosperous members of society.

10 Conditions to Create a Culture of Prosperity

4 ETHICS

INTEGRITY, HONESTY, AND ACCOUNTABILITY VS. CORRUPTION ARE CULTURAL VALUES AND PRACTICES

- Ethics and Integrity multiply a culture of prosperity because they support the work of CREATE OWN GROW.
- Corruption is a cancer that eats away the prosperity of a community because it destroys the efforts of CREATE OWN GROW.

5 HUMAN EQUALITY

- Every person has an equal opportunity to practice the Principles of CREATE OWN GROW.

6 THE RULE OF LAW

- Good laws are made in an open and fair democratic process and equally enforced on everyone.
- The Rule of Man does not prevail. Individuals in power do not get to break the laws to benefit themselves or to create laws that apply to others and not to themselves, or visa versa, for their own benefit.

7 PROPERTY RIGHTS

- There is a fair and simple pathway to purchasing property.
- One's legally owned property is protected by the courts from confiscation by the government or theft or misuse by others.
- A property owner may sell his/her property.

8 LOW TO MODERATE TAXATION

AND REGULATION ON THOSE WHO CREATE OWN GROW

- Taxes are low to moderate and government provides good services and infrastructure with that taxation.
- Regulation is low to moderate and fair.

10 Conditions to Create a Culture of Prosperity

AN EASY PATHWAY
TO LEGAL BUSINESS OWNERSHIP, REGISTRATION, AND TAXATION

9

- It is easy to legally start a business and register it with the government.
- The taxes imposed on business are low to moderate, produce good government services and infrastructure, and they are worth the benefits of operating a business openly and legally.

INFRASTRUCTURE
THAT SUPPORTS CREATE OWN GROW

10

- Education
- Health Services
- Transportation
- Financial Services
- Communications
- Wifi and Technology Access
- Utilities: water, power, sewer, trash collection and disposal

Ask Yourself

- How can I help others learn these 10 conditions?
- How can I organize people to work for these conditions?
- How can I influence my local political leaders to work for these conditions?
- Could I help a good political candidate who believes in these conditions get elected?
- Would I run for office to work for these conditions to create a culture of prosperity?
- What are the top 3 conditions that need improvement in my community?
- Which of these 3 is my #1 priority now?
- What is a good plan to improve this first condition as soon and as effectively as possible?
- Do I have the leadership resolve to get this done?

Testimonials

Maddo's Story

Maddo Owino grew up in a poor village in East Africa. Her mother passed away when she was young, and her father was an oppressive man. She became, in essence, the domestic slave who cared for her father and siblings as a child.

She rose daily before sunrise to fetch water, gather firewood, and prepare a breakfast of porridge for her father and siblings. Then she would head off to school. She would return at noon and then at dinner time to prepare meals for her family, then head back to school. She was often caned for being late to school. Some days she just skipped school to avoid the beatings.

When she was old enough, Maddo was able to go to college, but the job opportunities did not allow her to fulfill her destiny.

She attended PPI's CREATE OWN GROW training in 2014, where she listened carefully and took detailed notes. She left determined to apply the PPI Principles and Practices.

She started a health supplement sales business, and she grew a team of sales people. She started a café. That was natural for her because she had been cooking for groups all her life. Then she started a catering business that can and has fed up to 5,000. That's amazing. I only know two people who have fed 5,000 people at a time; Jesus and Maddo!

Guest House in Ahero, Kenya

Then she developed a beautiful two-story guest house with her family members to host tourists and mission teams. She has purchased business property in a country where only 2% of the property is owned by women.

She has purchased a car in a community where few women drive. She recently partnered with one of her employees to purchase a 3+ acre property for an agriculture business. She also supports orphans and ministries in her community.

I trained some of her employees and some people she was trying to recruit into her businesses in 2020. She is a PPI Certified Trainer, and I am very proud of Maddo for her work to CREATE OWN GROW.

Testimonials

George's Story

George Kienga, from Awendo, Kenya, was frustrated because he could not make enough as a teacher and a farmer to support his family. In 2012, he attended PPI's CREATE OWN GROW training in Nairobi, Kenya. He was a quiet, unassuming man, but he left determined to go home and to put what he learned to work.

First, George started with what he had. He started being more intentional in running his farm as a business to create the best value he could.

Then, again, he started with what he had. He had the ability to teach, and he started a preschool for the children of the farmers in his area. He started in a little tin metal shack on the corner of his property. He charged a small tuition to feed them and to teach them. The next year, he added a first-grade class at his school. He kept adding a grade per year.

He also started teaching the farmers in his community how to improve their farming to make more money so they could pay the tuition to send their children to his school. He has created 25-plus jobs for faculty and staff at Golden State Academy and more for his farms. Golden State Academy has grown to 380 students in grades K through 8th grade, and he plans to keep expanding through high school.

They have 80 boarding students. One hundred three of their students come from extreme poverty where they would often have days where they did not eat. At Golden State, they eat every day, and they are learning to become economically empowered as they grow up. Amazingly, Golden State is self-supporting. Their resources are meager, but they keep creating value. Golden State has ranked #1 in academic testing in their county for the last three years. They are the Flagship School of PPI which means:

- It was the first school founded on PPI Principles.
- It was the first school to teach our PPI curricula that will go to thousands of schools globally.
- We will help them develop their campus and resources so their students can become the leaders of solving poverty in Africa.

Today, George owns three sugarcane farms, 6 acres, 3 tractors and harvesting trailers, and he contracts for harvesting. And he has built a new house for his family.

Golden State Academy. Future Leaders of Africa

Testimonials

Shem & Jared's Stories

Shem Okello and Jared Okello have been strong Christian leaders in Kenya for a long time. They are models of men who are practicing CREATE OWN GROW and changing the future of Kenya.

Jared realized the best value he could create was in running for office and leading his county and nation in good policies and governance. After facing a corrupt election process which he lost, and fighting that corruption all the way to the Supreme Court, he then won his election bid to become a Member of Parliament for the Nyando District. Jared is leading change for the better in Kenya.

After Shem attended PPI's CREATE OWN GROW training, he began to put the principles to practice in an even greater way than he had before.

CREATE:
- He continued to create value in the ministries where he gives leadership.
- He continued to create value in generating new businesses.

OWN:
- He bought property and had a house built for his family.
- He bought property and had a three-story apartment building built. He is now looking at adding parking and more apartments next door.
- He co-bought a property for a bed and breakfast for tourists in Western Kenya.
- He bought property and built low-rent housing for university students.
- He co-developed the Guest House in Ahero with his family.

Shem and Joyce Okello and their children in front of their new home.

GROW – Here are some businesses Shem has created.
- Property Rentals
- Medical Clinic
- Tourist transportation
- Ladies Hair Salon
- Meat Market
- Chicken Business
- PPI Training

Jared Okello, Ronna Jordan and John Morgan.

Testimonials

Brian's Story

This is Brian's Story in his own words…

I was very young when my father abandoned my mother, younger brother, and me. Having no way to support us, my mother left us, too. Different people took us in until we got older, and then we had to survive on our own on the streets as orphans.

A few years ago, I met Maddo Owino, who is a Sales Director for Tiens, a food supplement company. She saw potential in me and brought me in as a member of her sales team. I have done very well in this position, and when John Morgan of People Prosper conducted a training workshop, she encouraged me to attend.

I am now a Certified PPI Trainer and have started teaching the course in Kenya in Kisumu and Mombasa. Maddo and I also recently partnered together to start a vegetable farm, and our first crop of sweet potatoes are ready to sell. From the profits, we are going to expand the business, and I am also saving money to purchase a home. My long-term goals are to have one of the largest agriculture businesses in East Africa and to empower unemployed youth with the PPI wealth creation principles.

I am thankful to John Morgan for bringing CREATE OWN GROW to Kenya and making it possible for an orphan to succeed in spite of life-long challenges and obstacles.

Brien Otieno, Maddo Owino and Shem Okello tasting the first crop of sweet potatoes from Maddo's and Brian's 3+ acre agriculture project.

Testimonials

Brenda, Tabitha, & Dorothy's Stories

Brenda is five, and her brother is in 7th grade. They are orphans that have been taken in by Golden State Academy.

Tabitha is six. She is an orphan who was malnourished when she was taken in by Golden State Academy.

Dorothy is eleven. The Kienga family took her in after George rescued her from her mother who was trying to kill her. She wants to be a doctor and is a motivated student at GSA.

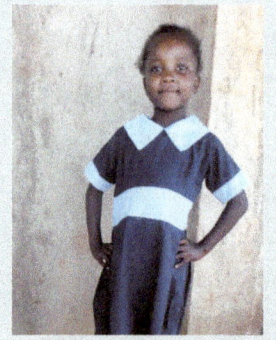 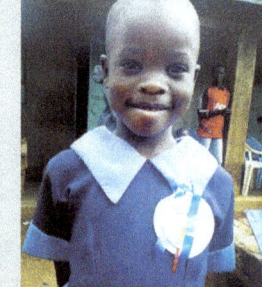

(left) Brenda. (right) Tabitha.

Dorothy.

Golden State Academy Girls

Testimonials

Jeffrey, Excellence Moses, and ATH

Jeffrey Ferezy and Excellence Moses Gichuho attended a PPI Empowerment Sunday at Parklands Baptist Church in Nairobi, Kenya in March of 2020. They say it changed their lives.

(left) Jeffrey Ferezy. (right) Excellence Moses Gichuho.

They were both recent college graduates who could not find jobs. So, they started a PPI Training business called Afrika Transition Hub to teach young Africans to be more competitive in a tight job market and to become entrepreneurs.

They are now key partners with PPI. They have been contracted by the Kenyan government to train Government interns to help them become better interns and to help them transition into the job market when they leave their internships.

They are partnering with several universities in Kenya to teach PPI Courses with college credit.

They are also partnering with Barclays and Equity Banks in Kenya who are sponsoring their Empowerment Workshops for Women.

They have a vision to empower one million young Africans in Kenya and across the continent of Africa to gain better jobs, to have better careers, and to start good businesses and organizations that will change the future of Africa.

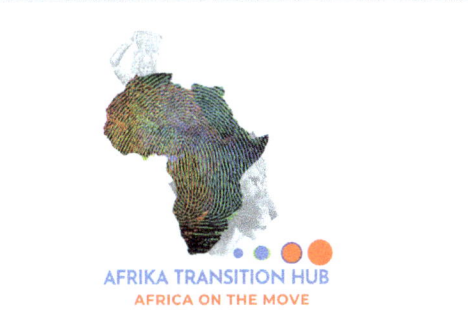

Afrika Transition Hub Training for Universities In Nairobi in March of 2021

Let's Create the Best Value

from p. 9

What are my strengths & abilities? _____
_____

Which can help me create the most value? _____
_____

from p. 10

I will use _____ in order to _____.
       (Which ability, talent, and skill?)   (Which need do I want to meet?)

from p. 12

What possession of others have I been envying? _____
_____

What value would I love to create? _____
_____

from p. 14

What are the best talents and abilities that I have? _____
_____

What is the biggest need that people have that I would most like to meet?
_____
_____

What knowledge and skills would I be willing to learn to be able to do this?
_____

VISION: Describe what my life could look like one year or more in the future if I pursued these things. _____
_____
_____

AMBITION: Describe the value I would like to create for others and that I would be creating for myself and my family with better income.
_____

Notes: Create

MY ACTION PLAN: What are the three main action steps I will take in the next few years to make my vision and ambition happen?

- Step 1: _____
- Step 2: _____
- Step 3: _____

p. 14 cont.

What knowledge and skills do I need to learn next? _____
_____
_____
_____

from p. 16

HOW TO START A BUSINESS OR SIDE HUSTLE

1. Identify my strengths and talents: What can I do well? _____
_____

2. Identify what I want to do: What kind of work do I want to do? _____
_____

3. Identify a need that people have: What will people pay for? _____
_____

4. Pick a business that fits my talents and desires and a need people have.
_____

5. List some skills and things I have that I could use to create value.
_____
_____
_____
_____

from p. 18

CREATE OWN GROW | 44

Let's Own the Best Property

from p. 21

What kind of property do I want to own? _____
_____

from p. 22

When will I plan to own property? _____

Am I creating the best value I can to create the best income I can? If not, revisit the Create content of this book (Pages 7-18, 43-44). _____

Am I budgeting my spending to control it? If not, I will create a budget and use it.
_____
_____

from p. 23

How can I create value from my home? Growing a garden? Raising livestock? Conducting Business? Renting a portion of it to tenants? Home improvements? Home expansions? _____
_____
_____
_____

from p. 24

What property maintenance and improvements do I need to do? Make a list

_____	_____
_____	_____
_____	_____
_____	_____

Let's Grow the Best Business

Which one of these business options fit my skillset and passions the best? *from p. 27*
_____
_____

What is my Unique Value Proposition? *from p. 28*
_____
_____

Where will I do this business and when?
_____
_____

How will I get the supplies and resources I need?
_____
_____

How will I get people to help?
_____
_____

How will I let customers know about my business?
_____
_____

How can I improve my people, products, services, and solutions? *from p. 29*
_____

What is working elsewhere and how can I do it better?
_____
_____

What new products, services, and solutions can I create?
_____
_____

How can I expand my business capacity? Add key people? Add equipment? Add more space? Add a new location in a new market?
_____
_____

CREATE OWN GROW | 46

Let's Create a Culture of Prosperity

from p. 36

How can I help others learn these 10 conditions?

How can I organize people to work for these conditions?

How can I influence my local political leaders to work for these conditions?

Could I help a good political candidate who believes in these conditions get elected?

Would I run for office to work for these conditions to create a culture of prosperity?

Notes: Culture of Prosperity

What are the top 3 conditions that need improvement in my community?

_____
_____
_____

Which of these 3 is my #1 priority now?

_____
_____
_____

What is a good plan to improve this first condition as soon and as effectively as possible?

_____
_____
_____
_____

Do I have the leadership resolve to get this done?

_____

Go Forth and Conquer

Left to right: Danny and Kelly Anglin and Greg Lanee' and John Morgan. Kelly made this art piece and it was presented to me by Pinon Hills Community Church.

Our children were young when the Principles of CREATE OWN GROW were coming together in my heart and mind.

The image in my mind was how God "blessed" the human race in Genesis 1:27-28. He created us in His image, then He told us to go forth in the world and be people who were fruitful and multiplying and mastering the resources He had created to make the best value we could. I thought of it as God saying, "Go forth and conquer!"

So, when our children would leave our house to go to school or to work, we would often say to them on their way out the door, "Go forth and conquer!" We meant you are created in God's image. He has given you special talents and abilities, so go forth and create the best value you can. We are blessed to see how they have done just that in their educations, careers, and ministries.

Now, it's how I close every teaching session where we are explaining the Principles of PPI. So, as we wrap up this book, let me say it to you… **Go Forth and Conquer!**

Notes: Culture of Prosperity

What are the top 3 conditions that need improvement in my community?

_____
_____
_____

Which of these 3 is my #1 priority now?

_____
_____
_____

What is a good plan to improve this first condition as soon and as effectively as possible?

_____
_____
_____
_____

Do I have the leadership resolve to get this done?

_____

Go Forth and Conquer

Left to right: Danny and Kelly Anglin and Greg Lanee' and John Morgan. Kelly made this art piece and it was presented to me by Pinon Hills Community Church.

Our children were young when the Principles of CREATE OWN GROW were coming together in my heart and mind.

The image in my mind was how God "blessed" the human race in Genesis 1:27-28. He created us in His image, then He told us to go forth in the world and be people who were fruitful and multiplying and mastering the resources He had created to make the best value we could. I thought of it as God saying, "Go forth and conquer!"

So, when our children would leave our house to go to school or to work, we would often say to them on their way out the door, "Go forth and conquer!" We meant you are created in God's image. He has given you special talents and abilities, so go forth and create the best value you can. We are blessed to see how they have done just that in their educations, careers, and ministries.

Now, it's how I close every teaching session where we are explaining the Principles of PPI. So, as we wrap up this book, let me say it to you... **Go Forth and Conquer!**

www.ingramcontent.com/pod-product-compliance
Lightning Source LLC
Chambersburg PA
CBHW081510080526
44589CB00017B/2720